Gustav Mahler

SYMPHONIES NOS. 5 & 6

IN FULL SCORE

DOVER PUBLICATIONS, INC.
New York

CONTENTS

Published in Canada by General Publishing Company, Ltd., 30 Lesmill Road, Don Mills, Toronto, Ontario.

Published in the United Kingdom by Constable and Company, Ltd., 3 The Lanchesters, 162–164 Fulham Palace Road, London W6 9ER.

This Dover edition, first published in 1991, is an unabridged republication of *Symphonie No. 5 für grosses Orchester*, C. F. Peters, Leipzig, 1904, and *Sechste Symphonie für grosses Orchester*, C. F. Kahnt Nachfolger, Leipzig, 1906. A glossary of German terms and lists of instruments have been added. We are grateful to the library of the Aaron Copland School of Music, Queens College, for the loan of one of the scores for reproduction.

Manufactured in the United States of America
Dover Publications, Inc., 31 East 2nd Street, Mineola, N.Y. 11501

Library of Congress Cataloging-in-Publication Data

Mahler, Gustav, 1860–1911.
    [Symphonies, no. 5, C♯ minor]
    Symphonies nos. 5 & 6 : in full score / Gustav Mahler.
    1 score.
    Reprint. Originally published: Leipzig : C.F. Peters, 1904 (1st work); Leipzig : C.F. Kahnt Nachfolger, 1906 (2nd work).
    ISBN 0-486-26888-8
    1. Symphonies—Scores. I. Mahler, Gustav, 1860–1911. Symphonies, no. 6, A minor. 1991.
M1001.M21   no. 5   1991   91-756905
                                              CIP
                                                M

GLOSSARY OF GERMAN TERMS

ab, off
abdämpfen, damp
aber, but
absetzen, remove
abwechselnd, alternating
abwogend, ebbing
acht, eight
Achtel, eighth-notes
alle, all
alles, everything
allmählich, allmählig, gradually
als, as, than
altväterisch, old-fashioned
am, on the, to the
A-moll, A minor
an, to
andere, other
Andern, others
Anfang, beginning
angehalten, slow
anhaltend, slower
Anmerkung, note
Art, manner
atmen, breathe
auch, also
auf, up, in the air, on, auf G, on the G string, auf und abwogend, surging and ebbing
aufgestellt, located, played
Ausdruck, expression
ausdrucksvoll, expressively
ausklingen, die away
ausschlagen, beat, conduct
äusserst, extremely

B, B-flat
bedächtig, deliberate, slow
bedeutend, significantly
befestigt, attached
beginnend, beginning
beiden, both
belebend, more animated
belebt, animated
beruhigend, becoming calmer
beschleunigend, accelerating
bestimmt, marcato
bewegt, agitated, bewegter, more agitated

bezeichnet, indicated
bis, up to, bis zum, until the
Bogen, bow(s), Bögen, bows, Bogen-wechsel(n), change(s) of bow
brechen, arpeggiate
breit, broadly, breiter, long

Dämpfer(n), mute(s)
das, the
dasselbe, the same
dem, the
den, the
der, the, of the
des, of the
deutlich, clear, distinctly
d.h., that is
die, the
Dirigenten, conductor
Doppelgr., double stop
drängen, hurrying, drängend, stringendo, pressing, speeding up, drängender, faster
drei, three
dreifach, in three
dreinfahren, plunging forward
drittem, drittes, third

eben, just
eilen, hurry
ein(e), a
einem, one, Einem, one player
einhaltend, restrained
einmal, once, noch einmal, once again
einzelne, individual
Empfindung, feeling
energisch, energetically
Entfernung, distance
erste, ersten, erster, erstes, first
Es, E-flat
etwas, somewhat

Fermate, fermata
Ferne, distance
festhalten, keep
feurig, fiery
Flag., harmonics
fliessend, flowing, fliessender, more flowing
flüchtig, fleeting

flüssiger, more flowing
folgt, follows
freihängend, suspended
frisch, lively, brisk
für, for

ganz, quite
ganze, whole
gänzlich, completely
gebrochen, arpeggiated
gedämpft, muted, muffled
gehalten(er), slower
gemessen(em), measured, gemessener, more measured
gemessigt, measured
gepeitscht, whipped
gerissen, cut off
geschlagen, struck, played
geschliffen, slurred, legato
gest., gestopft, bouché
gestrichen, bowed
gesungen, singing
get., geteilt, divisi
(mit) Gewalt, violently
gewöhnlich(e), ordinario, normal
gezogen, bowed
gleiche, same, even
grell, strident, shrill
Griffbr., Griffbrett, (on the) fingerboard
grosser, large
grösster, the greatest
gut, well

Halbe, (beat) half-notes
Hälfte, half (of a string section)
Händen, hands
Hauch, breath
Hauptzeitmass, main tempo
heftig, vehemently
hervortretend, prominent
hier, here, von hier an, from here on
hoch, high
(in die) Höhe, up, in the air
Höhepunkt, climax
höher, higher
Holzrand, wooden edge
Holzschl., wooden mallet
Holzstäbchen, wooden stick

im, in the

immer, always, steadily, still, *immer noch*, still, *immer Halbe ohne zu drängen*, steadily beating half-notes without hurrying

in, to

innigster, most heartfelt

ins, to

keck, brazen, impudent

klagend, plaintive

klingen, ring, *klingen lassen*, let ring

Kondukt, cortege

Kraft, strength, *kräftig*, vigorously

kurz, short

lang(e), long

langsam, slow, *langsamer*, slower, ♩ *etwas langsamer wie im letzten Takte* ♩, ♩ somewhat slower, like ♩ in the preceding tempo

lassen, let, allow to

leidenschaftlich, passionately

letzten, preceding

m., with

Mal, time

markato, marcato

markig, precise, marcato

mässig, moderato, *mässigend*, moderating

Mediator, plectrum

mehrere, several

mehrfach, several

militärischer, military

mit, with

möglich, possible

nach, in the, to, *Es nach E*, retune E-flat to E

nachlassend, slowing

nächsten, next

nächstfolgenden, following

natürlich, ordinario

nehmen, take, change to

nicht, do not, not, *nicht mehr*, no longer

nimmt, take, change to

noch, more, still, *noch stärker werden*, becoming yet louder, *noch ein wenig*, slightly more

nur, only

offen, open

ohne, without

Orchester, orchestra

Paukenschlägel(n), timpani mallet(s)

Pauker, timpanist(s)

Pause, pause

plötzlich, suddenly

Pulte, desks

rascher, faster

rein, precisely

Resonanz, près de la table

roh, *roher*, rough, raw

ruhig, calm, *ruhiger*, calmer

Saite, string

sammeln, gather

Satzes, movement

Sch., *Schalltr.*, *Schalltrichter*, bells (of wind instruments)

Schlägel, mallets

schlagen, beat, conduct

schleppen, drag, *schleppend*, dragging, *ohne zu schleppen*, without dragging

Schluss, end

schmeichelnd, caressingly

schmetternd, blaring, cuivré

schnell, fast, *schneller*, faster

schon, still

Schritt, pace

schüchtern, timidly

schwach, weak, *schwächer*, weaker

Schw., *Schwschl.*, *Schwammschlägeln*, sponge mallets

schwer, heavy

schwungvoll, energetic

sechs, six

sich beruhigend, becoming calmer

sind, are

singend, cantabile

so, as

Sord., *Sordinen*, mutes

spielen, play, *zu spielen*, to be played

spring. Bogen, sautillé

stark, vigorously, *stärker*, more vigorously

Steg, bridge

steigern(d), increasing

stets, *stetig*, constantly, steadily

stimmen, tune

straffer, tauter

streng, strict (tempo)

Strich, bowstroke, *Strich für Strich*, détaché

stürmisch, violently

Takt(e), beat, tempo, *im Takt*, in tempo

Teil, part

teilen, divide, *nicht teilen*, unisoni

(mit) Teller(n), clashed

Ton, tone, *Töne*, tones

Trauermarsch, funeral march

Triole, triplets

Trommel, drum

u., and

übergehen(d), progressing, moving to

übernimmt, takes, changes to

und, and

ungefähr, approximately

unmerklich, (almost) imperceptibly

unten am Griffbrett, at the bottom of the fingerboard

Vehemenz, vehemence

verändern, changing

verklingend, dying away

verlöschend, dying away

viel, much

vier, four

Viertel, quarter-notes

von, by

vorher, previously

vorhin, previously

Vorschläge, grace notes

vorwärts, (pressing) forward

Wärme, warmth

wechseln, change

wenig, little, *ganz wenig belebt*, only slightly more animated

werden, becoming

wie, like, as, as though

wieder, again, back to

wild, wild

womöglich, where possible

wuchtig, heavy, powerful, *wuchtiger*, more heavily

wütend, furiously

zart, tenderly, soft

Zeit, time, *(sich) Zeit lassen*, allow time

zögernd, lingering

zu, at, to, too

zum, for the, to the

zurückhalten, slow down, *zurückhaltend*, ritenuto

zurückkehren, returning

zuvor, previously

zwei, two, *zweite*, second, *zwei oder mehrfach besetzt*, using two or more instruments

3fach, in three, *4fach*, in four

1., *2.(etc.)*, 1st, 2nd (etc.)

INSTRUMENTATION

Symphony No. 5

4 Flutes [Flöten]
   (Fl. 3,4 = Piccolos [Piccolo-Flöte, Picc.] 1,2)
3 Oboes [Hoboen]
   (Ob. 3 = English Horn [Engl. H.])
3 Clarinets (A,B♭,C) [Klarinetten in A,B,C; A-Klar.,
   B-Klar., C-Klar.]
   (Clar. 3 = D Clarinet [D-Klar.])
Bass Clarinet (A,B♭) [A-Basskl., B-Basskl.]
2 Bassoons [Fagotte, Fag.]
Contrabassoon [Contrafagott, Contraf., C-Fagott]
   (= Bsn. 3)
6 Horns (F) [Hörner in F, F-Hörner]
4 Trumpets (B♭,F) [Trompeten in B,F; B-Tromp.,
   F-Tromp.]
3 Trombones [Posaunen, Pos.]

Tuba [Basstuba, Tuba]
Harp [Harfe]
Timpani [Pauken]
Glockenspiel [Glockensp.]
Cymbals [Becken], attached to Bass Drum
Bass Drum [Grosse Trommel, Gr. Tr.]
Side Drum [Kleine Trommel, Kl. Tr.]
Triangle [Triangel]
Slapstick [Holzklapper]
Tamtam
Violins I,II [Erste, Zweite Violinen, Viol.]
Violas [Violen]
Cellos [Violoncelle, Vcelle]
Basses [Bässe]

Symphony No. 6

Piccolo [Kleine Flöte, Kl. Fl.]
4 Flutes [Flöten, Gr. Fl.]
   (Fl. 3 & 4 = Piccolos)
4 Oboes [Hoboen]
   (Ob. 4 = English Horn)
English Horn [Englisch Horn, Engl. Horn]
E♭ Clarinet [Klarinette in Es, Es-Klar.]
   (= D Clarinet [Klarinette in D, D-Klar.])
   (= C Clarinet [C-Klar.])
   (= Clar. 4)
3 Clarinets (B♭,A) [Klarinetten in B,A; B-Klar.,
   A-Klar.]
Bass Clarinet (B♭,A) [Bassklarinette in B,A; B-Basskl.,
   A-Basskl.]
4 Bassoons [Fagotte]
Contrabassoon [Contrafagott, Contraf.]
8 Horns (F) [Hörner in F, F-Hörner]
6 Trumpets (F,B♭) [Trompeten, F-Tromp., B-Tromp.]
3 Trombones [Posaunen]
Bass Trombone [Bass-Posaune]
Tuba [Basstuba]

Timpani [Pauken]
Glockenspiel
Deep Bells [Tiefes Glockengeläute] (two or more,
   unpitched)
Cowbells [Heerdenglocken, Heerdengl.]
Xylophone [Xylophon]
Bass Drum [Grosse Trommel, Gr. Tr.]
Triangle [Triangel]
Side Drum [Kleine Trommel, Kl. Tr.]
Cymbals [Becken, Beck.]
Slapstick [Holzklapper]
Tambourine [Tambourin]
Tamtam (deep) [Tam-tam (tief)]
Switch [Rute]
Hammer
2 Harps (reinforced in 4th mvt.) [Harfen]
Celesta (two or more if possible)
Violins I,II [Violinen, Viol.]
Violas [Violen]
Cellos [Violoncelle, Vcelle]
Basses [Bässe]

SYMPHONY No. 5
IN C-SHARP MINOR/D MAJOR
I
1. Trauermarsch

In gemessenem Schritt. Streng. Wie ein Kondukt.

Vier Flöten.

Drei Hoboen.

Drei Klarinetten in A.

Zwei Fagotte.

Contrafagott.

Sechs Hörner in F.

Vier Trompeten in B.

Drei Posaunen.

Tuba.

Pauken.

Becken.
Grosse Trommel.
Kleine Trommel.
Tamtam.

Erste Violinen.

Zweite Violinen.

Violen.

Violoncelle.

Bässe.

1

★ Vorschläge so schnell als möglich.
Grace notes as fast as possible.

* Vorschläge so kurz als möglich.
Grace notes as short as possible.

*) **Becken nach militärischer Art an der grossen Trommel befestigt.**
Cymbals, in military style, attached to the bass drum.

*) Einzelne gestopfte Töne sind mit + bezeichnet.

Individual bouché tones are marked +.

Unmerklich zu Tempo I zurückkehren.

Basses *not* an octave higher!

2.

keiue Triole!
Not a triplet!

Bedeutend langsamer *(im Tempo des ersten Satzes „Trauermarsch").*

Etwas langsamer *(ohne zu schleppen).*

SYMPHONY NO. 5 (II)   99

*) Rit.=d. h. Kraft zum nächstfolgenden Accent sammeln.
Rit.: that is, gather strength for the following accent.

II

3. Scherzo

*) Vorschläge so kurz als möglich.
  Grace notes as short as possible.

114   SYMPHONY NO. 5 (III)

NB. Die Violinen dürfen die Holzbläser nicht decken.
NB. The violins must not cover the woodwinds.

*) Anmerkung für den Dirigenten: In diesem Motiv ist das Achtel stets etwas flüchtig=nachlässig auszuführen, in welches Instrument es auch gelegt ist; also ungefähr so:

Note for the conductor: In this motive the eighth-note must always be played somewhat fleetingly and carelessly, in whatever instrument it appears; thus approximately as follows:

Anmerkung für den Dirigenten. *11 Von hier an a tempo
Note for the conductor: From here on, *a tempo*

NB. Anmerkung für d. Dirig: die Holzharmonie darf vom übrigen Orchester nicht „gedeckt" werden.
NB. Note for the conductor: The woodwind section should not be "covered" by the rest of the orchestra.

Unmerklich drängend.

III

4. Adagietto

5. Rondo-Finale

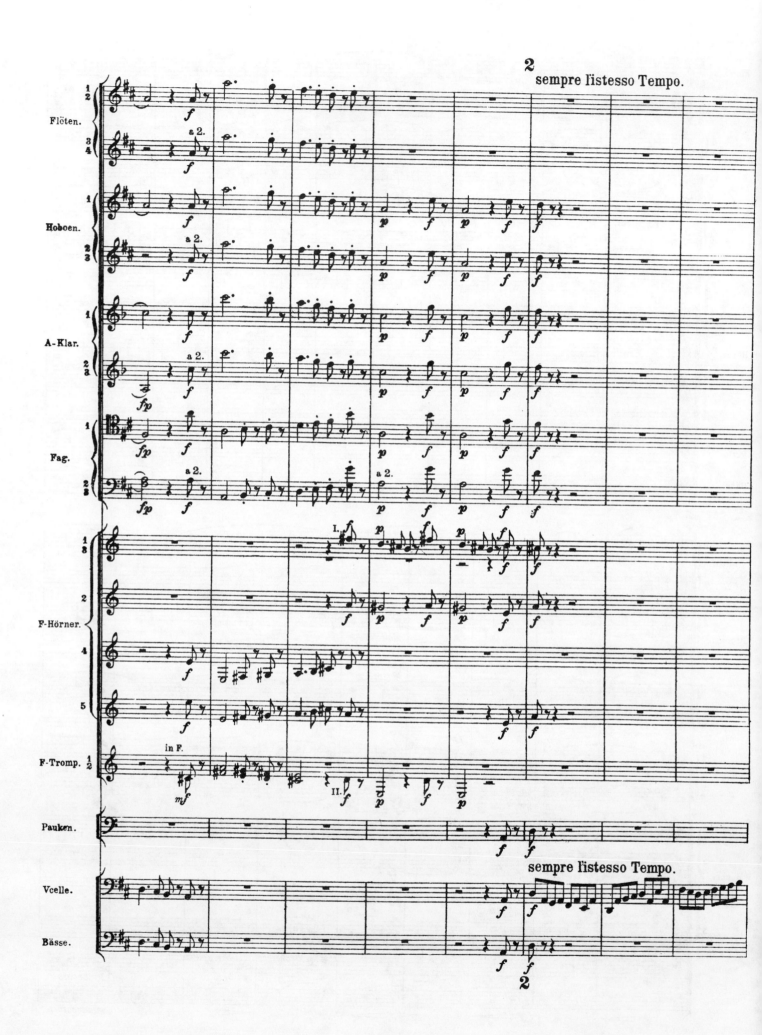

sempre l'istesso Tempo.

Unmerklich etwas einhaltend.

31 Allmählich und stetig drängend.

SYMPHONY No. 6
IN A MINOR
1.

*) Einzelne gestopfte Töne sind mit + bezeichnet.

Individual bouché tones are marked +.

N.B. Ein solcher Strich ＞＜ zwischen 2 Noten bedeutet
stets portamento (gliss.)

N.B. A stroke such as \ or / between 2 notes always signifies
portamento (gliss.).

N.B. Die *ten.* haben hier die Bedeutung eines *kleinen Haltes* mit vorausgehender geringfügiger Beschleunigung.
NB. The *ten.*'s here signify a brief pause after a preceding slight acceleration.

2. Scherzo

Plötzlich wieder, wie zuvor (altväterisch).

3.

SYMPHONY NO. 6 (III)   383

4. Finale

*) Zwei oder mehrere sehr tiefe Glocken von unbestimmtem aber von einander verschiedenen Klang, in der Ferne aufgestellt und leise und unregelmässig geschlagen.

Two or several very deep bells of indeterminate but differing sound, placed in the distance and struck softly and irregularly.

*) Das Es der 1. Posaune ist richtig.

The E♭ in the 1st trombone is correct.

*) Kurzer, mächtig, aber dumpf hallender Schlag von nicht metallischem Charakter.

Short, powerful, but dull-sounding stroke of a *nonmetallic* character.

Noch etwas drängender.

Kl. Flöte.
Flöten. 1. 2. 3. 4.
Hoboen. 1. 2. 3. 4.
D-Klar.
A-Klar. 1. 2. 3.
A-Basskl.
Fagotte. 1. 2. 3. 4.
Contraf.
F.-Hörner. 1. 3. 5. 7. / 2. 4. 6. 8.
F-Tromp. 1. 2. / 3. 4. 5. 6.
Posaunen. 1. 2. 3. / 4.
Basstuba.
Pauken.
Kl.Tr.
Becken.
Erste Viol.
Zweite Viol.
Violen.
Vcelle.
Bässe.

in F.

(roh)

(roh)

a 2.

a 4.

mit Paukenschl.

sempre ff

* Das *C* der Trompeten ist richtig.

The C in the trumpets is correct.